PRAISE FOR

Nancy Ross Hugo and Windowsill Art

❧

"Nancy Ross Hugo's *Windowsill Art* is visual poetry. I love this book and all it represents – a 'slow flowers' practice for the naturalist, gardener, and artist. As I read her text and studied her photographs, I jotted down words like inventive, vivid, wild, spare, subtle, quiet – a moment, a gesture, a ritual."

— Debra Prinzing, author of *Slow Flowers* and *The 50 Mile Bouquet*

"*Windowsill Art* leads you to the Zen of flower arranging – 'in the moment' inspiration from simple, ephemeral, unexpected beauty."

— Frank Robinson, President and CEO, Lewis Ginter Botanical Garden

"What could be better than a windowsill full of garden treasures ready for their close-up? Nancy Ross Hugo's *Windowsill Art* shares the joy of gathering garden ingredients to enjoy up close and personal. It's time to get rid of those dusty African violets and bring something fresh into your home."

— James Augustus Baggett, Editor, *Country Gardens*

"Nancy Ross Hugo can take a tattered autumn leaf, prop it in a vanilla bottle, and suddenly the eye is filled with beauty we might otherwise have missed. And she makes you realize you can do it, too. The best kind of book!"

— Phyllis Theroux, author of
The Journal Keeper and *California and Other States of Grace*

"Nancy Ross Hugo 'gets' nature. She steps outside, and, without relying on florist or grocery store flowers, she creates beauty from what she finds."

— Cheryl Lenker, Host, "The Master Gardener Hour" on America's Web Radio

Windowsill Art

Windowsill  *Art*

Creating
one-of-a-kind natural
arrangements to
celebrate the seasons

Nancy Ross Hugo

st. lynn's
press

PITTSBURGH

Windowsill Art
Creating One-of-A Kind Natural Arrangements to Celebrate the Seasons

ISBN-13: 978-0-9892688-5-1

Library of Congress Control Number: 2014940984
CIP information available upon request

First Edition, 2014

St. Lynn's Press . POB 18680 . Pittsburgh, PA 15236
412.466.0790 . www.stlynnspress.com

Book design – Holly Rosborough
Editor – Catherine Dees

Photo credits:
Author photo on page 177 © Robert Llewellyn
All other photos © Nancy Ross Hugo

Printed in Canada
On certified FSC recycled paper using soy-based inks

This title and all of St. Lynn's Press books may be purchased for educational, business, or sales promotional use. For information please write:
Special Markets Department . St. Lynn's Press . POB 18680 . Pittsburgh, PA 15236

10 9 8 7 6 5 4 3 2 1

For John,
my partner in everything

Cobalt blue bottles filled with zinnias sparkle when lit from behind. Light streaming through the window creates shadows, highlights, and other effects unique to windowsill arranging.

TABLE OF CONTENTS

INTRODUCTION

The simple pleasure of dropping a flower into a vase is multiplied when you drop more than one flower (or leaf, or seed structure) into more than one vase. Plant materials displayed here include a mottled red leaf, tickseed sunflowers, sumac foliage, avocado, Queen Anne's lace seed structures, sweet gum leaves, and grapevine foliage.

Almost everybody does it: puts a little something on the windowsill to watch it ripen, root, or just sit there looking pretty. It's such a great space, this little wooden platform that connects the outdoors to the indoors. As an avid flower arranger, I've begun to think of it as something like a Japanese *tokonoma*, the place where natural materials (and other objects) are displayed for artistic appreciation. But it's even more than that for me. The windowsill offers a place for practicing an art form that distills the essence of floral design and captures the joy of simple flower arranging. It provides opportunities for deep looking, for celebrating the seasons, and for playing with plant material. I don't want to describe it as a stage, because that implies something done for public admiration. Instead, I see it as a place where I can practice the art of displaying and combining plant materials without fear of censure and where the anxiety sometimes associated with formal floral design is absent.

As both a teacher and a student of floral design, I can say without hesitation that I have had more fun and learned more from creating windowsill arrangements than I have from creating thousands of more formal arrangements. For me, windowsill arranging is almost a spiritual practice. When I am looking for materials to display and placing them on the windowsill, I feel more like a poet placing words in a haiku than a floral designer placing stems in a vase. I love the limited space, the double connection to the outdoors (through the window and my materials), and the structure that repeating the same activity over and over provides.

I'll describe other rewards of windowsill arranging in the chapters that follow, but here let me emphasize that I think this activity is as beneficial and enjoyable for experts as it is for beginners. For amateur flower arrangers (and for those who don't aspire to even that title), windowsill arranging is a perfect way to bring nature indoors without the effort or expense of creating centerpieces or other elaborate arrangements. (Beware, though: it can be a gateway experience, generating enthusiasm for all kinds of floral design!) For experts,

it can be a path back to the kind of innocence and beginner's eye that most of us had at the start of our arranging careers. And it can help focus a lifetime of practice and observation. I once heard the author of a vegan recipe book, who was not a vegan herself, explain why she had written a vegan cookbook. She said that she limited her universe in order to investigate a small part of it more deeply. For her, writing a vegan cookbook was like an artist who usually paints in oils exploring pen and ink drawing. Windowsill arranging can be to floral design what pen and ink drawing is to oil painting: a way to strip the art form to its basics and distill the essence of it.

When I first dropped a pansy into a vase as a child, I may not have known what was motivating me, but I now know that when I display natural materials on the windowsill, I am celebrating nature, learning to see better, and sometimes creating something exciting that didn't exist before. It's a process that requires no special equipment, no fancy plant material (roadside weeds often work best), little time, and no teachers – but over the three years that I posted my windowsill arrangements online, I realized there is some value in showing other people what you are displaying on the windowsill. Over and over, people commented that I was increasing their degrees of freedom by showing them things they hadn't thought of, like using leftover collard ribs as arranging greens, displaying radishes upside down, and tying vases together with bindweed.

In *Windowsill Art,* I'll describe some of the materials, techniques, and practices that have made windowsill arranging more revealing, and enjoyable, to me. I hope they do the same for you.

Nancy

ONE

GETTING STARTED

My husband organizes a fall retreat around the ripening of Osage orange fruit (the grapefruit-sized green orb on this windowsill). Osage oranges are October touchstones for me, too, but I like to remember what else is going on outside when they are falling. The rose hips are turning red, for one thing, and that's worth celebrating on the windowsill.

Windowsill arranging uses the platform of a windowsill to showcase seasonal plant materials in jars, bottles, small vases, and other vessels. Just line up the containers and start dropping garden gleanings, snippets from florist flowers, roadside weeds, or other natural materials into them. It's that simple, but the rewards of this easy activity are enormous. For one thing, the limited space of the windowsill forces you to think small, so your arrangements

Although this combination looks autumnal, April brought these materials together. The red maple helicopters were hanging from a tree near the garden where the cilantro was sending up mature shoots.

audiences), windowsill arrangements are unpretentious affairs created in a less public spot (often over the kitchen sink) where the creator is the primary "audience." And who doesn't feel more free to experiment in private than in public?

Windowsill arrangements can be as exquisite as arrangements done for state dinners – or even more exquisite – but because of where they sit and how relatively temporary they are, they are never so "precious" that you're unwilling to shuffle their materials or rearrange them just for the fun of it.

Because they are so easy to create and change, windowsill arrangements are catalysts for creativity. It might take hours of work and many dollars'-worth of plant material to refurbish or recreate a large, formal centerpiece, but you can tweak, or totally replace, a windowsill display at no expense in minutes. And since it involves so little time, money, and effort, windowsill arranging encourages you to stay involved in the process and experiment over and over again. Why does no one ever emphasize the fact that in order to be creative you've got to be involved in something?

don't take long to create and require very little plant material. Small flowers and leaves that would likely be overlooked in larger arrangements or in the garden show to particular advantage on the windowsill. Another advantage of windowsill arranging is that it allows you to experiment with no penalty. Unlike arrangements done in the middle of dining room tables for guests (i.e.,

Creativity doesn't spring from a void; it arises when you are actively puzzling over something, or manipulating something, or playing with new combinations, or trying to fix something that didn't work the first time.

I don't approach windowsill arranging with the purpose of being creative; I'm just looking for ways to display plant material that keep it alive, showcase its beauty, and maybe reveal something interesting about its form, color, and character that I hadn't noticed before. When something new – something creative – evolves from the process, it isn't that I'm so creative; it's that I'm trying so many things, it's almost inevitable something novel will occasionally result. I subscribe to Linus Pauling's suggestion that "the best way to have a good idea is to have lots of ideas." And, if plant material is your artistic medium of choice, you'll find windowsill arranging one of the best ways to generate lots of ideas about how to use it.

The view out the window becomes part of the composition. Here, a red geranium, picked from a plant over-wintering in the house, stands out against a cold, foggy background.

An interface with nature

Windowsill arranging also provides lots of opportunities for guilt-free gazing out of the window. It's strange the way, after a while, we seem to stop looking out of the windows of our homes, but when you're arranging on the windowsill the backdrop (the scene out the window) almost insists on being seen. In some cases – I must put a red flower in front of that gray, foggy background! – it even becomes part of the composition.

I am sure I have witnessed many more subtle shifts in weather, movements of light and shadow, and changes in the gardens outside my windows than I ever would have if I hadn't been windowsill arranging. I refer to this as "window-pane time" as opposed to the "screen time" we spend in front of computers. When you arrange on the windowsill, you are arranging in front of a changing background, and sometimes it's like having a movie, a light show, and a

A handsome gin bottle serves as vase for this graceful branch of red-berried tea viburnum *(Viburnum setigerum).*

wildlife exhibit all contributing to your creation. When a cardinal perches on the fence outside my window or a luna moth hugs the screen behind one of my arrangements, I absolutely do consider it part of my arrangement, because I have chosen to arrange in a place where there is this dynamic interface between outside and in, between what I control and what nature adds.

Narrow windowsill? No Windowsill? No problem.

Occasionally, people tell me that their windowsills are too narrow for windowsill arranging, or, more rarely, that they have no windowsills at all. Not to worry; there are ways to experience most of the benefits of windowsill arranging without having a window. First though, if your problem is just a narrow windowsill, I'd look for containers with bases narrow enough to fit on it. A vanilla extract bottle has a base that requires very little real estate, and it is one of the very best vases for windowsill arranging. If you have no windowsill at all (or a windowsill you're not allowed to fill with plant material), consider designating a small shelf or tabletop for your arranging activities and keep practicing there.

The crucial thing is to choose an area with a relatively easy-to-clean horizontal surface (it could be a kitchen counter) where you feel comfortable displaying plant material, where the surroundings help limit the size and complexity of your arrangements, and where you feel free from judging eyes. Away from the window, you won't experience the backdrop benefits of working on a windowsill – you won't have the lighting and views that provide an extra dimension to windowsill art, but you'll still reap the rewards of regular creative practice.

These vases represent a wide range of styles and colors, but they have one thing in common...

CHOOSING CONTAINERS

Windowsill arranging requires no pricey equipment, just a few small containers and some plant material. Use small jars, bottles, vases, or other vessels from yard sales, antique shops, or the neglected shelves of the pantry. Good options include vanilla extract bottles, hot sauce bottles, cruets, retired salt shakers, even liquor bottles – anything that holds water and has a base narrow enough to fit on a windowsill will work.

...all of these vases have wide bases and narrow necks, which makes them perfect for windowsill arranging.

Vase shape

You can choose vases of any shape, but there is one shape that works so well for windowsill arrangements that you'll want to have a few on hand. It's a vase with a broad base and narrow neck – a shape that works particularly well for arrangements that include only a few stems. Such a vase is stable (with water weight at the bottom) and it will hold a small number of stems upright without their listing (the narrow neck providing them little wiggle room).

To understand why this works so well for arrangements that include only

This small vase is the little black dress of windowsill arranging; it is the perfect foundation for whatever else you might add.

a few stems, consider the alternative – a container with a wide mouth and narrower base, which is the shape of most collecting buckets and too many vases (whose designers must be using collecting buckets as their model). A vessel with a wide mouth and narrower base is the perfect shape for a collecting bucket; you can drop lots and lots of stems into it without their flower heads bumping into each other. It's a tricky shape for a vase, though, because it's top heavy and often requires many, many stems to fill it up. Much better, for those of us who don't want to spend all day

arranging or use stabilizing materials like floral foam, are containers with narrow necks and broad bases, which can easily display a few stems gracefully. You can certainly use wide-mouthed containers on the windowsill, and I sometimes do, but as a rule it takes more time, effort, and material to fill such containers than it does to display material in a container with a narrow neck.

Vase style and color

The style and color of your vases can be as idiosyncratic as you are. Because I usually want the focus to be my plant material and not my vases, I do most of my windowsill arranging in simple containers of clear glass or pottery in neutral colors. Sometimes a flower calls for a jazzier vase, or an unusual container so interests me that I want to use it as a focal point, but it's the simple, neutral-colored or clear glass containers that I use over and over again. They don't compete with my plant material, and they take one decision – finding a container of the appropriate color – out of the process.

It's nice to have a collection of containers in various sizes, so you can choose the one that suits the size of your plant material, and it's even nicer to have a collection of containers of various sizes that are all in the same visual family (all glass, or all earthenware, for example), so you can put a group of them on the windowsill at the same time. The consistent style of the containers can run like a theme through your display, helping to unite the plant materials.

Choose containers that fit the style and color of your home... or not. The containers I use on my kitchen windowsill most every day complement my kitchen (which is itself pretty spare and neutral-colored), but, because this is just a windowsill and not a mantel in the White House, I feel free to break loose and drop something outlandishly out of character onto the windowsill occasionally. For example, cobalt blue is not a color that looks particularly good in my house, yet I like blue bottles, so I sometimes use them on the windowsill.

This array of summer flowers has the appealing variety of a cottage garden; like a path through the garden, the matching containers provide an organizing aspect.

Flowers from forced paperwhite narcissus bulbs combined with mustard and moneyplant leaves create a wintry mix in cobalt blue bottles.

And although they suit the style of my nineteenth-century home not at all, I like to experiment with sleek, modern containers. The windowsill is, after all, a place to experiment, so I can use a shiny metallic cylinder one day and a homespun pewter pitcher the next if I want to.

FINDING PLANT MATERIAL

It doesn't take much to fill windowsill containers, and you'll be surprised how easy it is to find interesting material to use once you start scanning the yard, garden, neighborhood, and roadside. (Collect only what is legally yours or unequivocally free-for-the-gathering and abundant, of course.)

Seeing with new eyes

It's not just living materials you'll find useful for your arrangements. Consider colorful leaves that have fallen to the ground and other natural gifts that are shed from trees and shrubs, like twigs, fruit, cones – even bark. Once you've begun to see its windowsill potential, plant material on the ground of your yard, park, or playground begins to seem less like debris and more like free art supplies.

Where else could you look for inspiration? Common wildflowers and vines (especially the ubiquitous bind-weed) provide materials for windowsill arrangements, as does greenery pruned from shrubs and trees. Not everyone enjoys scavenging, but for those who do, those piles of yard waste the town recycling truck is going to pick up from in front of your neighbors' houses on Monday can be fine sources of arranging materials for you on Sunday. Don't pass them by unexamined. And weeds can be as dramatic as expensive florist flowers. I value the firework-like seeds heads of wild sedge more than most any purchased plant material I can think of.

Because I am an avid gardener, garden gleanings contribute enormously to my windowsill arrangements, but I seldom go outside with the goal of picking for the windowsill. Instead, I use a snippet or two from some plant that caught my eye as I was weeding, leftovers from deadheading, greenery pruned from

A circling root provided the inspiration for this arrangement. A cocktail skewer topped with a duck holds the root in place.

shrubs, and sometimes plant material I've pulled up or cut off by accident. That flower you snipped by mistake when pruning something else can become the focal point of a windowsill arrangement.

I've even rescued roots. One of my all-time favorite windowsill arrangements began with a thick, spidery okra root that was just too extraordinary to toss in the compost heap. Another organized itself around the root of a pot-bound plant that had twisted itself into a knot. Washed and dried, some roots last as long as sticks and are equally valuable because they can be used over and over again.

Because small mate-rials show up so well there, windowsills also make great places to display very small flowers,

like wild violets. Because you are arranging for yourself and not a paying customer, you can also use flowers and leaves that don't last very long. They are short-lived in a vase, but I absolutely love displaying snowdrops and crocuses on the windowsill, where they bring the thrill of early spring indoors. In fact, lots of the little bulbs that show up only en masse outside perform like headliners when displayed singly on the windowsill.

Bark rescued from a burn pile is displayed here on a plate stand.

13

In Defense of Short-lived Materials

A florist would never use a crocus as a cut flower, because it's so short-lived, but a windowsill arranger would.

Commercial florists and cut-flower growers value flowers with long vase life the way misers do money. Small wonder, since many of the flowers they use must travel long distances and purchasers want things they buy to last as long as possible. But when you're arranging for yourself, and have access to flowers that don't last very long once cut, there's no reason not to use them. If we can spend hours preparing a meal that lasts only an hour, why can't we create floral arrangements that last only a day or two (or less)? Using flowers and greens with short vase life increases your degrees of freedom enormously, and, when I want to, I may even use a stem or leaf out of water, knowing its beauty will be temporary. It's all a matter of balance – your time, your reward, your attachment to a particular material and how intently you're going to watch it. Some materials last so long you can get tired of looking at them (chrysanthemums come to mind); others die so quickly once cut that some people wouldn't bother arranging with them, but I can't imagine not using a daylily or morning glory because its bloom lasts only a day. To me, the very ephemeral nature of such flowers makes them more worthy of intense viewing, not less.

The kitchen windowsill is the perfect place to display vegetables, herbs, and fruits. Above are squashes combined with black cayenne peppers and dill.

Other sources of materials

Although I love the fact that most people can create windowsill arrangements without buying flowers, there is no reason you can't use florist flowers in windowsill arrangements if you want to. You certainly don't need to buy much, though. You could create scores of windowsill arrangements from one bunch of mini-carnations or spray roses purchased at the grocery store, and a florist's castoffs would be almost overwhelming to a windowsill arranger. Remember, though, that one of the purposes of windowsill arranging is to keep you in touch with the seasons, so locally gathered material is always best. If you use purchased materials, use them sparingly and combine them with seasonal, local materials.

Castoffs from other arrangements you have created yourself can supply windowsill materials, too. As arrangers collect plant material for large arrangements, they usually remove the lowest leaves and flowers so they won't be under the water level (where they would rot and foul the water). These usually wind up in the trash or compost heap, but you can recycle them for use in windowsill arrangements.

Mixed peppers, eggplant, and basil fill this low green container.

You can also raid your houseplants for arranging materials. I have a bedraggled angel-wing begonia I'd have thrown out years ago if I didn't enjoy using it as a "donor plant." Another example: if you have a fern over-wintering (or living permanently) in the house, it can be a great source of arranging greens.

Among my favorite materials to display on the windowsill are fruits, veggies, and gourds. I confess I grow some peppers and squashes more to look

Here, I've displayed a radish in one vase and fennel tied up into a harp shape in another.

A spice jar filled with basil and blackberry lily flowers accompanies tomatoes on this windowsill.

at them than to eat them. You can actually do both: look at them for a while in the windowsill and then eat them! Putting fruit in the windowsill to ripen is something most everyone does, and windowsill arranging just builds on that. Instead of lining them up like bowling balls, you can position them on top of vases, stack them like logs, even arrange them like flowers. I once read about a young woman who lived for a year on nothing but the fragrance of lavender. Okay, that was a myth, but I do think I could live for a while on just the sight of vegetables.

Cooking provides another source of arranging materials, and some kitchen scraps have so much visual interest they deserve life on the windowsill before being discarded. I felt like Leonardo da Vinci the day I discovered that the ribs of collards I used to throw away (the center parts from which you trim the leaf flesh) looked like green feathers and stood up beautifully in a bottle on the windowsill. To my surprise, I also found these "feathers" will last weeks in water.

Although I'm not as thrifty and devoted to "freegan" arranging as these recycling activities might suggest, I do think the ease of finding free plant material to display in the windowsill is one of the advantages of this activity. In fact, I enjoy the process of discovering interesting materials to display as much as I do the arranging itself.

The feather-shaped "leaves" in this arrangement are actually collard ribs. The darker green leaves are mountain laurel.

Best Materials

The materials that work best in your windowsill arrangements will depend on where you live and what outdoor areas you frequent. I live in the mid-Atlantic region of the U.S. and have access to a wide range of plant material all year, but if I had access to only the following four plants (or plants with similar personalities), I think I could come up with a windowsill arrangement every day. Here are the four plants I consider staples, and why.

Common, easy-to-grow nandina provides leaves, flowers, berries, and even interesting twigs for windowsill arrangements, but its most useful gift to windowsill arrangers is its leaflets. They can be culled from the shrub's larger compound leaves, which emerge copper-colored in spring, turn green in summer, and turn shades of red and burgundy in fall.

Pansies (as well as smaller-flowered violas and wild violets, *Viola* spp.): Pansies provide flowers in a wide range of colors and bloom in early spring, late fall, and sometimes even mid-winter, when many other flowers aren't available. Their scale is right for windowsill arrangements. Heart-shaped leaves of wild violets are also really useful, because they provide contrast to more complicated flower and leaf forms.

Nandina *(Nandina domestica)*: Nandina provides flowers, berries, and leaves, all of which look beautiful in windowsill arrangements. Nandina leaflets, which can be snipped from the larger, compound leaves, are particularly useful and have a simple, oriental look that adds elegance to the humblest vase. (The oriental look should be no surprise; nandina is native to east Asia). My only reservation in recommending nandina is that it can seed into North American native plant habitats, where it is inappropriate. Remove it there.

Okra: Okra is easy to grow and, to my mind, deserves as much room in the cutting garden as it does in the vegetable garden. Leaves, buds, stems, pods – all are useful in windowsill arrangements. I find myself using the same dried okra pods over and over again in windowsill arrangements. The flowers are beautiful, too, although each flower lasts only a day.

Fern: I love the linear, graphic look of a fern frond, and for some reason a single fern frond adds elegance, and a sense of naturalness, to any windowsill display. If you don't have ferns growing in your yard or woodland, you can harvest from ferns growing as houseplants or from outdoor potted ferns.

A single bracken fern frond lights up the windowsill when framed against the night sky.

Ramble Arrangements

Here's a challenge: see if you can create an entire windowsill display using nothing but plant materials you find along the path or roadside you walk. This

I collected this plant material, and even the bottle, on a walk one winter morning. The materials include red oak leaves, Christmas fern, Japanese honeysuckle, sweet gum leaf, greenbrier, loblolly pine needles, and red oak leaves.

is obviously easier if you walk along rural roadsides lined with weeds and wildflowers than it is if you walk in an urban or suburban setting, but even there, you can find fallen leaves, discarded plant parts, and windfalls that provide great arranging material. On my walk, which includes rural roadsides and railroad embankments, I can even find containers for arranging, and there is satisfaction galore in creating something from a weed and a soda bottle.

TWO

EXPLORING THE PROCESS

Even tall flowers, like snapdragons, will stand upright in short, narrow-necked vases if you provide them some support. Here I've stuffed snippets of loosestrife leaves and leftover snapdragon stems into the necks of the vases to keep the snapdragons from listing too much.

If ever there were an activity proving the process is the product, windowsill arranging is it. It's not the creation of particular arrangements that I find most exciting, it's knowing how they evolved and seeing how a leftover material from one display can become the centerpiece of another. Almost never do I have a pre-formed image of what I'm going to do when I start playing with plant material on the windowsill, but just by being involved in the process, things happen.

I've tried to think of ways to make this sound harder, but I can't! At the risk of sounding like a weight-loss coach, I promise that if you follow these three easy steps, you'll succeed.

Step one: Place a container or collection of containers on the windowsill. Once you have them in place, your brain can start imagining what might fill them and nature will start delivering it. This is a classic case of "whatever you're looking for, you will find." Empty vases are like magnets – they draw things to them.

Step two: Fill your container with water, drop your natural material into it, and, if necessary, fluff it up. A friend once told me that she belonged to the "drop it in and fluff it up" school of floral design, meaning she just dropped her flowers into a vase and "fluffed them up" until their orientations and heights suited her. With windowsill arranging, "fluffing it up" isn't even always required, but if your stems don't stand the way you want them to stand or your flowers don't face the way you'd most enjoy them, "fluff them up" (meaning reposition or reorient them). Adding additional material (it won't take much if you're using a narrow-necked container)

or tucking discarded stems into the neck of the vase will help you position your materials where you want them. If your featured material needs another stem to prop it up or make it look more dramatic, add it. And if you don't like this combination or the materials' relative heights and orientations, change them. Trust your instincts. If there really are certain proportions (like the divine proportion) that are universally pleasing, you should be able to discover them with your eyes, without a course in aesthetics.

Step three: Repeat. Repeat this process until you have a collection of vessels filled with seasonal natural materials on the windowsill. Now repeat again, and again, and again. As material wilts or dies, replace it. As you grow tired of one material and enamored of another, throw the first one away and replace it with the second. Because this is just a windowsill display (not an arrangement of pricey materials for an exacting audience) you can be as fickle and profligate as you want. And you can change your containers when you want to, too.

COMBINING AND SHUFFLING MATERIALS

Once you start playing with flowers, leaves, cuttings, you'll discover that you're seldom beginning from scratch. Instead, you're removing dead materials and adding fresh ones to vases that may already contain a long-lived plant material. Windowsill displays evolve over time. Some materials die quickly, others live a long time, and over the course of their vase-lives, the long-lived ones may keep company with a variety of recently-added materials. This makes for interesting observing, because you get to see how many ways there are to display a single material and how pleasing the various combinations are. Hellebore leaves, Christmas fern fronds, nandina leaves, and poet's laurel foliage last a particularly long time, and I've used the same tiny snippet of cryptomeria

foliage – which is gorgeous and almost immortal – in combination with scores of shorter-lived materials over the course of four months.

A hellebore seedling (inadvertently pulled up while gardening) appears here in a pretty bottle next to a tiny vase containing a smaller hellebore leaf and a red maple leaf. I used the same red leaf in several arrangements, including the one on page 50.

Less is more

With windowsill arranging, remember to keep it simple. When I find myself adding more than three materials to a single vase on the windowsill, I know I'm heading into "regular" flower arranging territory and I try to rein myself in. Almost always, I find my simplest creations the most rewarding. My husband, who was once a carpenter, often quotes the funny carpentry line "I keep cutting and it's still too short." With windowsill arranging, I often realize "I keep adding things and it's still too complicated." Less is definitely more in the windowsill, and the best model for a windowsill arrangement is probably not the elaborate arrangements ladies take to garden club meetings but rather their horticulture exhibits – those bottles containing single flower or foliage specimens. With windowsill arranging, though, you can display whatever you want to, there are no judges, and nibbled leaves and petals are not only not disqualified, they are encouraged!

Once you've begun to bring plant materials inside and display them on the windowsill, you'll discover that some materials look more comfortable in one bottle, vase, or jar than another. So, in addition to trolling for plant material outside, you may find yourself looking for the appropriate container in which to display your plant material. I have a shelf in the basement where I keep all sorts of containers, but sometimes, it's a juice glass or a jelly jar in the refrigerator that seems best suited to my plant material.

A word about proportion

I think most everyone has an intrinsic sense of balance that helps inform such choices, but if you feel totally at a loss regarding how to match plant material and vase, consider the rule of thirds: in terms of visual weight, some say the proportion of plant material to vase should be $2/3$ to $1/3$ ($2/3$ plant material to $1/3$ vase). I find this rule more useful than rules that prescribe the proportion of plant material height to vase height, because it can be applied to horizontal as well as to vertical arrangements, but even this rule I use only as a guideline. More important, to me, is remembering that it is plant material, not vases that I want to display, and I don't want my vase to be so large or visually significant that it overpowers my plant material.

You can play with just one container on the windowsill at a time, or you can fill a series of them as materials present themselves. Don't worry if some of your containers remain empty. I enjoy seeing an empty container here and there in a windowsill display. It provides breathing room between flower-filled containers and suggests something about the possibility of what's to come.

If you're using narrow-necked containers, it won't take much to fill them, and every container can hold a different material or you can repeat materials across the windowsill. It's fun to drop the same material into each of several bottles, then add a series of different materials to accompany it. Or you can go out looking for materials of just one color and begin with those. The windowsill on page 28 started out

Two glass bottles – one empty – create a quiet but interesting environment for this 'Cinco de Mayo' rose. A simple vanilla bottle holds the striking rose.

as a collection of blue flowers, until the dogwood flowers insisted on being included. It's also fun to create a display of just one type of material – daffodils, tree leaves, or shrub buds, say – just to show how varied that single theme can be.

This started out as a display of blue flowers (woodland phlox, periwinkle, ajuga, Jacob's ladder), but white dogwood flowers muscled their way into the mix.

Connected glass tubes hold this lineup of April daffodils.

A container fashioned of three test tubes displays brown leaves and seed structures. The collection of brown materials was inspired by the tiny tulip poplar leaf on the right, which was a particularly rich chestnut brown color. I picked the nandina leaflet (left) and the seed structures of perilla and hardy begonia (center) because they were similar in color but different in form.

In this arrangement, the focal point is a purple pansy, the filler is pachysandra foliage, and trumpet vine serves as flagpole (albeit a weepy one!).

A flagpole, a filler, and a focal point

Another approach to windowsill arranging involves including a flagpole, a filler, and a focal point in each container (or in just one). This is my terminology for the elements often included in a traditional, upright flower arrangement, and I suggest it with some reluctance because you don't want your windowsill displays to become too contrived. On the other hand, I tend to gravitate toward this sort of mix even when I'm trying to keep things simple, and I think the three terms are really useful to beginning arrangers.

By flagpole I mean something linear that points up like a flagpole and often tapers to a point (sometimes with a wispy tip). Think grasses, willow wands, perennials with narrow, strappy foliage. A filler is something that fills in between the flagpole (or flagpoles, because there can be more than one) and the focal point (which is the visually dominant material in the vase). Most of the time, focal points are dramatic flowers, but they can be visually dominant leaves, fruits, or other materials. Fillers are usually leaves, but flowers – especially small, multi-branched ones – can function as fillers, too, as long as they're not too showy. In this sort of collection, the dominant material or focal point is traditionally placed low (relatively close to the lip of the vase) in the composition, and the flagpole (with its sometimes wispy tip) rises high. ("Wispy high, weighty low" is the way I explain this to Brownies.) The focal point can be weighty in the sense of sheer mass or because its form or color makes it visually dominant. In the crocus arrangement on page 14, the two daffodil leaves function as flagpoles, the crocuses as focal point, sweet box foliage as filler. Playing with this sort of arrangement – finding a flagpole, filler, and focal point for each vase – is fun and results in satisfying combinations that train your eye to appreciate form and "character" in the plants you encounter.

Whatever your approach, once you have some containers filled with plant material, observe and adjust the vases and their contents to suit you. Or, in the words of songwriter

The flagpoles here are Virginia thimbleweed, the filler is wild petunia foliage, and the focal point is wild petunia *(Ruellia)* flowers.

Here, black and white chopsticks serve as the flagpoles, peachy zinnias serve as the focal point, and hardy begonia leaves and stems serve as filler.

Paul Simon: "remove the irritants." In describing the process of songwriting, Simon notes that a large part of the work is just getting something down and then "removing the irritants." This is equally true of flower arranging and gardening. Tasha Tudor, famous for the color combinations in her flower borders, said the reason her combinations were so good was that whenever something came up that she didn't like, she removed it immediately. With windowsill arranging, "removing the irritants" is as simple as discarding any plant material, or combination of materials, you find unsatisfying (or ugly), but, as these other artists have discovered, you can't begin to remove irritants unless you first give yourself something to respond to!

PRACTICING

Think here of practicing not as some routine activity you engage in to master a task but rather as a spiritual practice that helps you discover new things (or see the old ones in new ways). That's the way windowsill arranging works: the more you do it, the more you see.

I have been creating a windowsill arrangement almost every day and posting it on my blog regularly for over three years, and I am absolutely convinced that the more you do it, the more you learn and the more fun it is. Posting my displays for an audience changes the process a bit (it introduces the contaminant of wondering if other people will like it), but the benefits of doing this regularly accrue to me as they do to everyone else. What you discover from really regular, disciplined, "I've promised myself I'll do this every day" windowsill arranging, is that your best ideas don't necessarily come on the days when you feel best or are looking forward to playing with plant material. Sometimes it's quite the opposite. And the displays that satisfy you most some-times evolve out of the ones you didn't like much. I wasn't far into my post-an-arrangement-a-day routine when I realized I was going to be posting things that didn't reflect particularly well on my skills as a flower arranger. Tough. But the routine also resulted in scores of arrangements that would have never occurred if I hadn't been playing in the windowsill so much, and many a favorite creation would never have been made without the raw materials from a less satisfying one.

My reality-checker tells me most people aren't going to create as many windowsill arrangements as I do, and that's fine, but I think you do need to create something new there at least weekly for the process I'm describing to work. If this seems like more than you can do, remember that you're not always creating something from scratch. As often as not, you're just pulling out spent materials, adding a few new ones, and shuffling the still-living old materials in with the new ones. The same piece of poet's laurel (a long-lived evergreen)

I seem to choose the same vase for hardy cyclamen flowers every October. I'm repeating myself, but then so are the cyclamens, so it's okay! Here, the cyclamen are combined with a sprig of Andromeda *(Pieris japonica)*. Notice the tree silhouettes reflected in the tile under the vase.

may stay in one of my containers for a month, and be combined with scores of different flowers, before I remove it.

Even more important than how regularly you practice windowsill arranging is that you do it year round. That's a must. Unless you live in the Arctic (and I fully expect an Arctic resident could show me how to do it even there), there is always some plant material worthy of display on the windowsill. I'm not sure I don't enjoy windowsill arranging more in the winter than I do in the summer, because I'm not so overwhelmed with choices. There's a kind of paralysis that sets in when you have too many choices, but in winter, the thrill of finding something you want to display is invigorating. Finding display-worthy material in winter is just a matter of adjusting your eyes to the landscape. Sticks, cones, seed pods, snippets from evergreens, tree twigs with beautiful resting buds (which will sometimes open in the warmth of the house), even mosses are great subjects for winter windowsill display.

When you practice windowsill arranging regularly, and do it year after year, patterns will emerge that reinforce your sense of the progression of the seasons. I used to worry that I was repeating myself when I found myself dropping a cyclamen flower into the same tiny green bottle every October, but now it feels almost like a rite of passage into fall, reminding me that, yes, another year has passed, and yes, the cyclamen are blooming on schedule again, and yes, I'm still here enjoying the same little flower in the same little bottle. It's actually sort of shocking how predictable blooming times are, and I love having a chance to celebrate such punctuality. You can set it up as a challenge to use materials like swelling maple flowers, stretching alder catkins, maturing okra pods, or blooming cyclamen in different ways each year, or you can enjoy the routine of repeating yourself. Either way, you'll be sealing memories and increasing your appreciation of natural rhythms.

Borrowed Windowsills

The window ledge at a beach cottage provided a platform for this single peony flower in an antique glass bottle.

If you happen to decide, as I did, that you want to practice windowsill art whenever the mood strikes you, no matter where you are, you may find yourself away from home and having to borrow a windowsill (and maybe flowers and containers, too!). Instead of being an impediment to your creativity, this can be a stimulant. Hotel windowsills can be challenging, because they are narrow (just prop the plant material up on the windowsill without container, if necessary), but trolling for plant material in these sometimes plant-barren environments can be fun. Use the rind from your breakfast grapefruit, weeds from the flower beds or pots by the entrance, or the parsley garnish from your club sandwich. Interesting containers may or may not be easier to find. A friend jokes that I had to drink the entire bottle of gin to get the bartender to give me the gin bottle I once used as a vase, but, in truth, it was almost empty when I spotted it on his shelf and he gave it to me without much resistance. Arranging at a rented vacation cottage also offers creative possibilities, because if any vases are available, they are probably not ones you'd have chosen yourself. All the more reason to use them! And if no vases are available, inventing them (from anything that holds water, like the toothbrush caddy) can be fun.

In another beach cottage, I found these unusual blue containers, which were fun to use because they were so different from what I use at home.

Sweet peas from the Fish Market provided the flowers and Subway cups provided containers for this windowsill arrangement in Seattle.

A coffee mug filled with roadside weeds graces this adobe windowsill in Santa Fe.
An unopened packet of coffee grounds hidden in the mug helps hold the weeds upright.

Finding Inspiration

More often than not, it is a striking flower, leaf, seed pod, twig, or fruit that drives my windowsill arranging. I encounter a natural material that moves me then start thinking about the best way to present it. Usually I just drop it into a nearby bottle or jar and let it stay there, with or without companion materials. But sometimes I am so impressed by a color combination or design that I encounter elsewhere (on a card, plate, or napkin, say) that I let that object drive my windowsill display. Other sources of inspiration include seed catalog covers, illustrations, scarves, and labels. Anything from which you take color or design inspiration can serve as a prompt for a windowsill arrangement.

Here is an arrangement I created after falling in love with a plate I bought at a local gift shop. Without the inspiration of the plate, I don't think I'd have had the courage to combine these particular oranges, pinks, and blues.

LETTING ARRANGEMENTS EVOLVE

From spotting an interesting piece of plant material outdoors to positioning it in a vase – even that short span of experience involves lots of choices. Which vase will I drop a flower into, which leaves or twigs (if any) will I use to support it, where will I place it among other items collected on my window-sill? But that's just the beginning of the windowsill arranging process, which reuses, recycles, and repurposes mate-rials with a regularity that would do the greenest eco-warrior proud. How this process evolves and how one learns to make the most of what's available are best described, I think, with examples.

The arrangement at right started on a November day when I was outdoors admiring leaves – especially the deep reddish-maroon leaves of a particular oak-leaved hydrangea. I picked a couple of them and took them inside where I decided they were too big to use in vases, so I positioned them under a small, clear glass vase. Then I went back outside looking for something to drop into the vase. I picked some red cedar foliage, thinking it wouldn't detract

The fall color of an oak-leaved hydrangea leaf provided the inspiration for this little arrangement, which also includes spirea foliage.

from my leaves, but when I put it in the vase, it didn't add anything to my arrangement either. Then I remem-bered some autumnal spirea foliage I'd seen outside, so I went out and picked a sprig. Loved it the minute I saw it in my hand, because of the graceful, open arrangement of its twigs. Still, the clear glass vase seemed to leave a gap between the spirea foliage and the oak-leaved hydrangea leaves, so I went trolling for a better vase. It's a miracle I happened to have this little deep-maroon vase on my shelf, because deep maroon is not my favorite color; the vase had been a gift from a friend, however, so I'd kept it. It proved to be perfect for these materials, so, voilà – a little windowsill arrangement I liked and enjoyed making.

The arrangements below evolved much less deliberately. I can't tell you how many times just dropping leftover plant material into the nearest water-holding vessel has resulted in a window-sill arrangement, and this is a case in point. After using some long fronds from a lady fern in a larger arrange-ment, I had some small pieces left over that seemed too pretty to throw away. I tossed them, temporarily I thought, into a wine glass sitting on the kitchen counter. But after putting a little water in the wine glass and lifting it onto the windowsill just to get it out of the way, I realized how wonderfully graphic the fern fronds looked silhouetted against the interior of the glass. So I made them

Leftover fern fronds launched these two arrangements.

even smaller and dropped them even deeper into the bowls of two different glasses. I really liked this simple arrangement (just fern fronds in two wine glasses), but a day or so later, as I was dismantling another arrangement, I found myself with a sasanqua camellia flower in my hand that also didn't want to be thrown away, so it wound up in one of the wine glasses with the fern.

Leftover apple peels were the catalyst for the arrangement on the right. I was about to throw them in the compost bucket when I realized their color and swirly shape were just too pretty to throw away.

Apples, apple peels, and spray roses create this great color mashup.

I dropped them into stemmed glasses where I enjoyed looking at them. Then I realized I had some peach-colored roses sitting in a bucket on the back porch (where they'd been sitting for days following an event for which I'd created large arrangements). I added them to the mix and loved this combination color-wise. Someone should name a play "Apples and Old Roses," because it's such a rich association – especially when there's apple cake baking in the background!

The evolutionary process that resulted in the arrangements on pages 44-47 could be called "Order from Chaos," because it started with the mess of foliage at right. If this doesn't look familiar, then you've never forced paperwhite narcissus bulbs and watched their foliage keel over toward the end of their reign. Still, the foliage is a beautiful spring green, and in January, when most people are throwing their spent paperwhites out, it's appealing to the spring-green-starved eye.

Sagging paperwhite foliage can be clipped off, straightened up, and reused in small arrangements.

Recycled paperwhite foliage, a round of almost-dead rose blossoms (left over from the arrangement on page 43), and a fatsia leaf create a striking combination – and this all started with the paperwhite foliage.

Shifting the fatsia leaf behind the round of roses created still another interesting way of looking at these materials.

I decided to salvage some of this foliage, and because what appealed to me about it, in addition to its color, was its linear form, I built on that by giving it a straight-up presentation in a vase composed of attached glass tubes. This linear display seemed to cry out for contrast, so I displayed a big, fat fatsia leaf beside it.

The next day, just because I had them, I decided to add the dying and drying roses I'd used in the arrangements on pages 46-47. But how? Because they were already drying out, I knew they didn't need water, so I jammed them into one of the boxes a round of brie cheese comes in. This added another graphic element to the preceding day's arrangement.

And finally, just for a change, on the third day these materials were in the windowsill, I pulled the fatsia leaf out of water and positioned the round of roses on top of it. Very dramatic!

Paperwhite foliage (left) and a fatsia leaf (right) provide a study in contrasts.

Knowing When to Stop

In a sense, you never finish working on windowsill displays, because you're always harvesting materials from old arrangements to create new ones, but I like to share a friend's advice about knowing when to stop fiddling with a particular arrangement. My friend, a painter, says you should stop working on a creative project when you are 80 percent satisfied with the results. Otherwise, she contends, you will waste time trying to get to 100 percent (time that could be better spent working on something new) or you'll ruin what you've already done. I've shared this advice with scores of students and friends who now call this The Eighty Percent Rule. I can't say that I always abide by it – sometimes getting to 100 percent is just too tempting – but I appreciate the wisdom of the advice. Alexander Calder also had a good answer to the "how do you know when you're finished?" question. Calder's answer: "When it's dinnertime!"

The gift of a great pair of socks provided inspiration for this display, and I was 80 percent satisfied with it the minute I dropped brightly-colored violas into these cereal bowls.

THREE

EXPERIMENTING WITH STYLES AND TECHNIQUES

I was just playing with this beet (displayed beside a jug of coleus) when I realized I could turn it upside down and support it on its leaf stems. This orientation showcases the part of the beet I like best – its tapering root.

Once windowsill arranging becomes a habit, your eyes become more alert to interesting plant materials, your hands more adept at handling them. You almost can't help having that happen. What takes longer is trusting that something exciting or creative or personally rewarding will result from your arranging practice, and I think I have the cure for that: change your perspective. You are not trying to make a work of art or create the perfect reflection of the season every day; you are trying to create a reflection of the season and you are engaged in learning what you like (with all the surprise that entails).

You truly can't fail at this if you view it as a process of discovery. Not every day will you have an "Aha! I like that!" moment, but the more windowsill arranging you do, the more satisfying moments there will be. First, there is the discovery connected with finding what you want to display – and second, there is the discovery of how you want to display it. The latter process includes looking for a container, deciding what to display alone, what materials to combine, when and what to shuffle. I love the not-knowing what will end up in the windowsill each day, the waiting to see what will evolve after I drop a few stems in containers, and the creative shuffling that continues for days after. Yes, a process this free-wheeling sometimes results in messes, but reorganizing a mess is sometimes part of the creative process.

My favorite part of practicing windowsill arranging is the fact that it is always experimental. I'm sure there are thousands of arrangers more skilled than I am, but not one of them explores exactly the same landscape I do and has the same light, today, on this particular windowsill where I alone am making creative decisions during this particular little nugget of time. What a luxury it is to get to play in this way! So…my prescription for successful windowsill arranging can be boiled down to one word: experiment. I can't tell you exactly what to do because your materials, your taste, and even your windowsill will be different from mine, but in the sections that follow, I'll share some of what I've learned in the hope it will expand your degrees of freedom.

A box of test tubes serves as "vase" for a single red maple leaf.

PLAYING WITH LEAVES AND VINES

It must be the genes we share with bees that make us more likely to focus on flowers than leaves, but leaves are among my favorite materials to display on the windowsill. And they needn't play second fiddle to flowers. Because the stage is small, a single, dramatic leaf can be as show-stopping as a vase full of flowers in another venue, and a

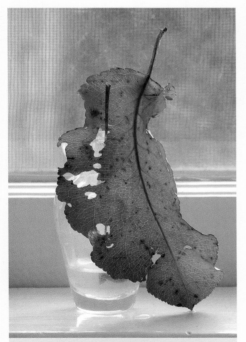

A stick through a hole in a tupelo leaf helps connect it to the tiny glass vase, providing it support.

collection of common leaves has the appeal of a rarity when displayed to advantage. The trick is to be on the lookout for interesting leaves and to give yourself permission to use them. Colorful fall leaves make obvious subjects for display, but you don't have to present them in obvious ways. I used to think I had to dry and press fall leaves before displaying them out of water, but I've observed that most of them will keep their shapes a few days before curling up, so now I feel free to use them straight from the garden or leaf pile. Sometimes I prop them up against vases, using the vases almost like easels, or I use them like doilies under my containers. You can also gather the stalks of leaves in your hand as if they were flower stalks and drop them into a narrow-necked vase exactly as you might a collection of flowers.

Leaves of vegetables and herbs also make great windowsill material. Left-over sprigs of basil and parsley often wind up in vases on my windowsill, and among the most dramatic leaves you'll ever display in the windowsill are fresh

Fall mahonia *(Mahonia bealii)* leaves look great in a Ball jar.

Backlight, like that passing through these bigleaf magnolia *(Magnolia macrophylla)* leaves, often adds drama to leaves displayed on the windowsill.

collard, mustard, kale, and Swiss chard leaves. Use them alone or combined with other materials.

Once you begin to appreciate the nuances of leaf color, shape, and texture, you'll start seeing leafy subjects everywhere. The leaves in the wine glass on the right came from the acalypha cutting on page 57. I was stripping leaves from the bottom of the cutting before dropping it into water to root, when I realized the leaves I was stripping off were too beautiful to discard.

Leaves "harvested" from the lower portion of a copper plant stem provided raw material for this concoction.

Ginkgo leaves look like ruffed collars when displayed in vanilla extract bottles with pyracantha berries.

I am also always on the prowl for skeletonized leaves – leaves that have been eaten and turned lacy by insects. They interest me from both an aesthetic and ecological point of view, as do leaves damaged by other animals or even disease. (Trying to figure out who or what did the damage becomes part of the leaf's mystique.) A perfect leaf can be beautiful, too, but, like the British artist Richard Bell (who memorializes imperfection in his nature journals), perfect things sort of leave me cold. Like Bell, who favors "a plant with a

54

Fresh curly kale leaves share the windowsill with honeysuckle and a rose.

A damaged leaf can be more artistically interesting than an unblemished one. A groundhog nibbled on this Swiss chard leaf, turning it into an *objet d'art*.

In this arrangement, I've combined single peonies with a Swiss chard leaf, tied upside down, to a glass bottle. Swiss chard leaves keep their shape a remarkably long time out of water, although if this radiator had been on, the leaf's "shelf life" would have been dramatically shortened!

story to tell," I like a leaf with a story to tell.

Other leaves you'll find useful in windowsill arranging belong to a category I call "large, simple-shaped leaves," although size is relative, and even the leaf of a violet can appear large in comparison to smaller things. A leaflet stripped from a complicated compound leaf can also function as a simple-shaped leaf. What you are looking for are leaves that are visually "unfussy"– they are uncomplicated in form and serve as contrast to more complicated materials (particularly those comprised of many small parts). Such leaves perform the same function in windowsill arrangements that they do in larger arrangements – providing simple backgrounds and contrast to

Light filters through copper plant *(Acalypha)* leaves the way it does through stained glass windows.

The leaves in the photo above are all relatively simple-shaped (with undivided blades). They provide nice contrast to more complex flowers and leaves.

The leaves in this photo are more complicated and will fight with equally complicated flowers (and each other) if combined too closely in small arrangements.

more visually complicated materials. The quintessential large, simple-shaped leaf is a hosta leaf, which arrangers treasure, but lots of other leaves, including those of ligularia, asphidistra, arum, and brunnera fit this description (as do ivy, heuchera, and violet leaves when used with smaller materials). Even an oak leaf can function as a large, simple-shaped leaf if you combine it with, say, a clutch of fussy asters.

I don't want to get too prescriptive about this – you certainly don't need a large, simple-shaped leaf in every windowsill array – but if you become alert to such leaves in the landscape and play with them in the windowsill, you'll notice how valuable they are, because we see things better in contrast, and combining fussy things only with other fussy things tends to generate a quarrel.

Vines

Vines also make great subjects for windowsill display, and there are myriad ways to use them. Because they want to hang, trail, twine, and twist, it's fun to let them do that. For example, you can let them trail along the windowsill between containers or lead them up sticks and other flagpole-like material as if they'd grown there. (When you find a stick or twig already encircled by a vine, resist the urge to pull it off, because you might want to display the entire ensemble in the windowsill.) Another way to display a vine is to let it hang from a vase positioned on the meeting

I put a vase on the meeting rail of this window frame so the passion flower vine could trail down.

rail (top edge of the lower sash of a double-hung window frame). This horizontal surface is not technically a windowsill, but it has most of the advantages of one, including limited space (so you can't go overboard with your arrangement), plenty of light, and

Bindweed wends its way through this collection of vases holding mandevilla flowers and greenery. Although it looks fragile, this common weedy vine holds up well in arrangements.

an outdoor background. Best of all, it allows you to let a good vine trail gracefully down in front of the lower sash without obstruction.

Some vines are also so malleable that you can twist them into shapes and postures different from those they took in the garden. Malabar spinach (a climbing annual vine), bindweed, greenbrier, Carolina jasmine, and other jasmine vines are particularly good candidates for twisting and twirling into interesting shapes.

In this arrangement, a Malabar spinach vine circles pansy flowers. Climbing Malabar spinach is easy to grow in the vegetable garden (or in pots), where it forms wonderful curves and swirls naturally, but it can also be twisted into most any shape you want.

Making Connections

If they have been collected locally, the materials in a windowsill display almost always share one trait: they reflect the time of year. But there are other ways to connect materials on the windowsill, too. You can connect them visually by displaying them in similar or identical containers. Repeating at least one natural material in each of several vases also makes the entire display look more "of a piece." The repeated material or vase works like a common thread or theme uniting the display. Placing an identical tile under each container adds even more coherence. You can also literally connect your arrangements by weaving vines between them. And one of my favorite ways to connect vases physically is to lay a woody vine horizontally across the tops of a series of vases, then drop stems of flowers and foliage into the openings between the vine and the throats of the vases.

By repeating the same plant material in a series of similar or identical vases, you multiply the visual impact of both. These three vases of yellow-flowered loosestrife are as arresting as triplets.

The woody material connecting these wooden spools is an old ivy vine stripped from a tree. I've dropped daffodils and periwinkle foliage through openings in its latticework–like construction. A floral tube in each spool provides water.

Roses, hydrangeas, and magnolia cones share a color palette, but the element uniting them physically here is a woody vine. I've laid the vine — from an arborescent ivy — across the tops of the vases and slipped the flower and cone stems though it.

BREAKING AWAY FROM BOTTLES

I seldom tire of using simple bottles and jars as vases, but sometimes an unusual container cries out to be used on the windowsill. And sometimes, the impulse to turn something that wasn't intended to be a vase into one is irresistible. The world is full of vessels that might be used as vases but aren't, and most anything can be turned into a water-holding container by lining it with something water-tight. Florists sell small, plastic tubes that can be slipped into small, otherwise leaky containers, and both test tubes and cigar holders (those made of glass and those made of metal) make excellent liners. When considering your windowsill arranging possibilities, let no object go unconsidered as a potential vase.

It's worth remembering that not everything you display on the windowsill requires water to keep it alive, so a vase isn't always necessary. Fruits and veggies can obviously sit on the windowsill out of water, and so can cones, dried leaves, nuts, nests, sticks, rocks, roots. There are also some materials that would be happier in water but can survive a while without it, so there's no reason not to enjoy them out of water for a while if you want to. Knowing this opens a new realm of possibilities – like suspending materials from the window lock or resting a hunk of mahonia directly on the windowsill.

Plastic cups stacked up for washing inspired this arrangement of marigold flowers and scented geranium foliage.

This spool of twine holds a daylily flower and black-eyed Susan bud. The flower and bud lasted only a day out of water – but that's as long as the daylily would have lasted anyway. Had I needed the black-eyed Susan to last longer, I could have inserted a water-holding floral tube into the top of the spool.

A wedge cut into this gourd provided entry for water and marigolds. To my surprise, the gourd (which was not a hard-shelled variety) proved water-tight. If you don't trust your gourd to hold water, line it with a floral tube or jigger. The gourd's little cap can perch above the flowers because it has been attached to a stick. First jammed into the bottom of the cap, the stick travels though the flowers into the bottom of the gourd.

These two materials – ginkgo leaves and pyracantha berries – captured my attention one October day, and when I brought them inside, I wanted to keep them together in the same way my eye had seen them outside – without an intervening vase. They looked prettier hanging together than lying together on the windowsill, so I hung them from the window lock. Without water, they did dry out, but they were gorgeous for several days.

On an October afternoon, my husband appeared at our front door bearing two gifts: an Osage orange and a turkey feather. "Maybe you can use these in a windowsill arrangement," he suggested. Oh, yes! I combined them by inserting the turkey feather into the Osage orange.

The Challenge of Horizontals

Using wide-mouthed, horizontal containers is more challenging than using narrow-necked, vertical containers, because positioning your materials where you want them is harder (no nice, narrow neck to provide support!). But there are ways to provide purchase to materials you want to display in horizontal containers. You can use floral foam or pin holders to help you position materials, or you can jam the vase full of some material, like red cedar, that doesn't rot quickly but does provide a grid of foliage and twigs into which you can drop other stems. Keep the red cedar below the lip of the vase and you'll never know it's there. Arrangements in horizontal containers don't themselves have to be horizontal, of course, but I tend to use them that way, not just because the mechanics are easier but because they seem to get my brain working in a horizontal direction. Sometimes, too, the process works the other way around:

A small nest of red cedar (which you can't see) provides support for pine needles, fertile fern fronds, and mint leaves in this horizontal container.

a material that seems to be asking to be displayed horizontally cries for a horizontal vase. See page 175 for my pairing of a gorgeous Japanese maple branch with a long, low vase.

Hibiscus holders also hold flowers in a horizontal position. These old-fashioned vases are sometimes made of clear glass, sometimes china, and they were designed to hold short-lived hibiscus flowers, but they work for all sorts of materials you'd like to display horizontally. They seem to defy gravity by holding water in a little pool that will accommodate an almost horizontal stem.

A single hibiscus flower looks great displayed horizontally in a hibiscus holder.

PROVIDING PLATFORMS
(AND OTHER ACCOUTREMENTS)

This delicate combination of 'Lipstick' salvia and asparagus foliage looks even more elegant sitting on a pristine linen napkin.

An easy way to add pizzazz to a windowsill display is to place your container on a tile or trivet. You can buy individual 3 by 3-inch tiles in various colors at home improvement stores for under a dollar, and it's fun to have a collection of these to place under vases. They enhance your arrangement by giving it a little stage to stand on. Napkins, swatches of cloth, flat rocks, small trays, and dishes can also provide interesting platforms. Sometimes, too, you may want to use trays or dishes as backgrounds for arrangements of flowers that are otherwise hard to see against the windowpane. By turning a tray or solid-colored dish on its side and securing it behind a vase (or putting it on a plate stand) you can provide a contrasting background. Obviously, this erases the beauty of light streaming through your materials, but that's some-times a trade-off you'd like to try.

If you want to add even more drama to your materials, you can stage them on platforms that lift them high above the windowsill. For example, instead of

A black tile anchors this black vase of daffodils, andromeda, and Scotch broom foliage.

A green tile serves as stage for this vase of wild violets.

placing fruit directly on the windowsill, you can display it on an upside-down wine glass, a narrow-necked vase, or a large wooden spool. The kind of wooden spool pictured on page 74 is fairly easy to find in antique stores and makes a particularly good platform. Plate and picture stands, like the one showcasing bark on page 13, also add "lift" to your materials and provide them a sort of star status as a result.

Another accoutrement that's really fun to play with when making windowsill arrangements is chopsticks. They come in a wide array of colors and designs and add a striking vertical element to small arrangements. As I mentioned in Chapter 2, they can function, in fact, like the flagpoles in "flagpole, filler and focal point" arrangements.

Another way to use chopsticks is to lay them in a grid pattern across a small bowl of water, then drop a relatively large flower (like a daffodil or camellia) into the square created where they intersect. Such arrangements are incredibly dramatic. If you don't have chopsticks to create the grid (or want to create a larger grid), use bamboo or straight sticks cut just a bit longer than the diameter of your bowl.

A mahonia leaf and a tile add interest to this vase of spray roses

The brown lid of an old wooden box provides background to these tiny white snowdrops.

This method of displaying large flowers draws attention to the intricacies of their blooms. Daffodils, camellias, and deciduous magnolia flowers look particularly pretty perched on a grid of chopsticks.

Green chopsticks add drama to this combination of small sunflower and 'Butterfly' holly. Notice, too, the yellow dish serving as a platform.

A single winged gourd sits on a wooden spool where its texture gets the attention it deserves.

FOUR

ARRANGING THROUGH THE SEASONS

The lushness of late summer reveals itself through (and on) this windowsill. The flower in the connected glass tubes is hardy begonia *(Begonia grandis)*, a perennial with foliage as beautiful as its flowers.

A reviewer of one of my favorite poetry collections, Ted Kooser's *Winter Morning Walks,* describes the power of Kooser's poetry as "accretive," a word I latched onto immediately as equally applicable to windowsill arranging. Even without his poems describing his walks, Kooser's precise descriptions of the weather each winter morning in Garland, Nebraska (cold!) worked on me like accumulating snow, increasing, by gradual addition, my understanding of his days.

Windowsill arranging is accretive in the sense that it gradually increases your sensitivity to natural beauty. When adopted as a routine, this personal, creative practice also builds creative muscle, because the more you experiment, the wider the universe of arranging possibilities becomes. But I find the most lasting impact of windowsill arranging, a benefit gradually accrued over time, to be in the insight it provides to seasonal change. The Chinese divide the calendar into twenty-four, not four, seasons, among them fortnights described as "excited insects," "grains fill," "cold dew," and "frost descends," and I love these descriptors because they allude to seasonal progressions more subtle than some grand change every four months. There are weekly, even daily, changes that windowsill arranging (or any practice requiring regular observation of nature) will alert you to, and it is the "accretive power" of observing those subtleties that I most value. As I write this, it is not just fall, it is a day in the second week of November when mulberry leaves have just fallen, gumballs are still green, daylily foliage is yellowing, roses are still throwing a few blooms, and white oak acorns are on the ground. Tomorrow there will be a different suite of phenomena to notice, but next year I'll probably see the same things again (and more!) in the same order.

If you are using materials from the surrounding landscape, your windowsill arrangements will always be a rendering of what is going on outside, and you can't help noticing patterns as you repeat the process over and over. I find it particularly rewarding to photograph

It was high summer in Massachusetts when I dropped this yellow wishbone flower (*Torenia*) into a borrowed coffee mug.

my displays, because the photographs serve as a form of nature journaling, reminding me what blooms when, which leaves unfurl first, which plants bloom, bud, or leaf out at the same time. also how the arrangements evolve and how the contents of one arrangement might get shuffled or recycled to form another. If they check the blog often enough, they also get to see my failures

> "IF YOU ARE USING MATERIALS FROM THE SURROUNDING LANDSCAPE, YOUR WINDOWSILL ARRANGEMENTS WILL ALWAYS BE A RENDERING OF WHAT IS GOING ON OUTSIDE..."

In fact, I am sometimes startled to look back at my photographs and realize that although I had been meaning to create something "pretty" every day, it is seldom the beauty or design success of an arrangement that moves me when I look back at the photos; it's the way they capture the seasons. I love being reminded how colorful the oak leaves are in November, how cheery the daffodils are in March, and how dazzling the daylilies look in July.

I've been told that some people like looking at my blog once a month (rather than daily) because it's like watching time pass. They notice not just changes in the plant materials but (or what I thought were failures at the time), but I've come to realize that as long as I'm practicing I'm learning, and I love the fact that, as of this minute, every arrangement I ever posted is still sitting on the Internet where anyone in the world can see it. If nothing else, this is a record of seasonal plant material in central Virginia, USA, planet earth, where there is so much to see and celebrate.

On the pages that follow, you'll find a sample of my windowsill arrangements organized by month. Be sure to look not just at the designs, but at how the backgrounds and materials change through the seasons.

Pine twig, cabbage leaf, arum berries, and geranium foliage.

Gumballs stacked on a decorative bowl.

Oak leaves tucked into the top of a wooden spool.

Brown eggs, tree-ivy leaves, boxwood foliage, papaya fruit (cut) and avocado rinds.

Alder twig, complete with catkins and cones, in brown bottle.

February

Cabbage leaves in bowl, Lenten roses *(Helleborus orientalis)* in vase.

'February Gold' daffodils, winter aconite flowers, and celery leaves in a sugar shell.

Arum berries with green stinking hellebore *(Helleborus foetidus)* floret and cyclamen leaf.

Periwinkle flowers and foliage nested in moss. A floral tube under the moss provides clean water to the periwinkel stems.

Nandina foliage and a sprig of chlorotic Virginia pine in an orange pitcher.

March

Sweet William, wild mustard, and Chinese temple bell *(Moricandia avensis)* flowers.

Pink camellia flower, aucuba foliage and twirled leaf from cast iron plant *(Asphidistra)* in wooden ikebana vase. Nested in the wooden vase is a pin holder, securing the stems in place.

Violas in stone cube with gumball.

Black pussy willow in connected glass tubes.

Yellow marsh marigolds and blue starflowers *(Ipheon uniflorum)*.

Eastern red columbine with pale yellow bishop's hat
(*Epimedium* x *versicolor* 'Sulphureum') flowers and jewels of Opar foliage.

Saucer magnolia flowers with Deodar cedar, mulberry, and heuchera foliage.

'Pickwick' crocuses combined with liriope foliage.

Early-blooming *Iris reticulata* with a single liriope leaf.

A lovely Lenten rose *(Helleborus orientalis)* in antique bottle.

Winter-weary *Mahonia bealii* foliage supported by wooden textile spool.

A mixture of daffodil and hellebore flowers, old leaves, and decorative bottles.

A glove, a pine cone, and the twig it was attached to – almost exactly as they came in from outside.

Gumballs and a spray of loblolly pine needles displayed in black pin cup with kitchen plate behind.

Early spring weeds and wildflowers (marsh marigolds, henbit, and hairy bittercress) in pearly-blue vase with terra-cotta backdrop.

The beautiful spring weed henbit looking elegant in a glass vase with china plate background.

A branch of dramatic dead leaves displayed in an old tin measuring cup.

April

Orange tulips with magenta sweet William, yellow wild mustard, lavender Chinese temple bells, blue periwinkle, and heuchera leaves.

Small cluster of Lenten rose *(Helleborus orientalis)* blossoms in vase on shed windowsill; Japanese kerria blooming outside.

Pale yellow daffodils and lavender violas in connected glass tubes.

Array that includes lily-of-the-valley, peony buds, snapdragon, blue woodland phlox, blue squill...

... plus iris, Byzantine gladiolus, and a few pieces of hosta and Jack-in-the-pulpit foliage.

The beautiful 'Annelinde' tulip with white-flowered money plant.

Alpine strawberries *(fraises des bois)*, grown by my neighbor Rosanne Shalf.

Chives in one vase, a radish straight from the garden in another.

Rose and wisteria flowers with broccolini seed pods, heuchera leaf, and other foliage.

Crimson clover and wild grasses nested in a Swiss chard stalk and balanced in a glass vase.

Single peony flower with a ruff of pine needles.

Bearded iris with comfrey flowers and foliage.

Buttercups with purple vetch, ragwort, and wild grasses.

June

Graceful garlic scapes combined with 'Frosted Explosion,' an ornamental grass.

Blanket flower *(Gaillardia)* in shot glasses with eleagnus, pine, and juniper.

Trumpet vine florets filled with white astilbe flowers and Japanese hakone grass.

Butter-and-eggs flowers with river oats on exterior windowsill.

A vibrant mix of zinnia, coxcomb, celosia, ageratum, and phlox flowers.

July

Red Meidiland roses with wisteria foliage.

Large dill seed head in recycled glass bottle.

Pattypan squash with black cayenne peppers and dill.

White garden roses on Maine windowsill.

Tomatoes and hot pepper on windowsill with basil in red vase.

Yellow crookneck squash with sunflower, elderberry flowers, and
a snippet of hydrangea foliage nested in it.

August

Sunflower, blackberry lily seed pods, basil, tansy, and marigolds in Neal Reed mugs.

Butterfly weed and yellow marigolds in one Neal Reed mug, ripening tomato perched on another.

Single okra leaf in tiny glass vase.

Trumpet vine flowers, seed pods, and foliage in inkwell and cruet.

Single stem of blue lobelia in contemporary vase.

Tomato perched on an overturned bowl, sunflower in striped green vase.

September

Nasturtiums, ironweed, celosia, and sweet peas combined in recycled glass bottles.

Tickseed sunflowers *(Bidens aristosa)* combined with Queen Anne's lace seed stalks.

Fall-blooming colchicum *(Colchicum autumnale)* flowers, hypericum foliage, and ornamental grass foliage.

Rustic boxes filled with an immature sunflower head (above) and stacked marigold blossoms (right).

This is a temporary display, but marigolds will last longer than you think out of water.

Mandevilla flowers and vines with holly fern and fetterbush foliage.

Dark, almost black, sweet gum leaves.

Wild morning glory flowers and foliage in an old, brown jug.

October

Fall-blooming camellias combined with fern fronds.

Pyracantha berries and white aster flowers in vanilla extract bottle;
pyracantha berries and yellow maple leaf in glass goblet.

Perennial helianthus flowers and poet's laurel foliage on a rainy day.

Mixed fall flowers and foliage including rose, chrysanthemum, zinnia, and 'Lipstick' salvia...

...as well as aster, snapdragon, and mandevilla.

Pansies and scented geranium foliage backed by a Japanese bamboo mat.

Nasturtiums and small marigolds in a Neal Reed mug.

November

Spools of trellising material with okra pods nested in one, yellowing peony foliage in another.

A bird's nest holding an Osage orange on a spool of trellising material.

Oak-leaved hydrangea leaves with spirea foliage.

Japanese maple and grass foliage with rose hips.

Fall oak leaves with ornamental gourd, pumpkin.

Zinnias with oak leaves and okra pods.

Sassafras leaves (three shapes) in glass vases.

December

Rose hips and pine needles gathered into a bouquet.

Pine needles inserted into pomegranate.

Stem of mottled greenbrier leaves in narrow vase.

Pyracantha berries and mint leaves in ball of twine. A floral tube
nestled inside the ball of twine holds water.

Paperwhite narcissus flowers with salad greens and winged begonia foliage in blue bottles.

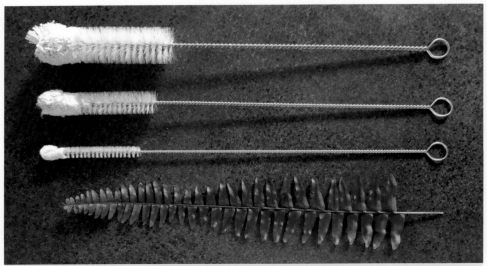

The one disadvantage of vases with narrow necks (the best kind to use on the windowsill) is that they are notoriously hard to clean. Look online and in gardening catalogs for small vase brushes like these.

The Arranger's Market specializes in hard-to-find, easy-to-use vases and other arranging equipment. You'll find many of the vases and other containers pictured in Windowsill Art on The Arranger's Market website (www.thearrangersmarket.com).

Lee Valley Tools (www.leevalley.com) offers a set of three vase brushes that are useful (if not essential!) for cleaning small vases with narrow necks – the kind I recommend for windowsill arrangements.

A.M. Leonard Horticultural Tool & Supply Company (www.amleo.com) sells Slimmer Trimmers, the best clippers in the world for everyday arranging and gardening activities. They are lightweight, sharp, and can be closed with one hand.

Seeds for many of the flowers and vegetables featured in *Windowsill Art* are available from the following sources:

Renee's Garden Heirloom & Gourmet Vegetable, Flower & Herb Seeds
(www.reneesgarden.com)

Southern Exposure Seed Exchange
(www.southernexposure.com)

Baker Creek Heirloom Seeds
(www.rareseeds.com).

Sometimes, hidden in the vase of one of my arrangements (especially a horizontal one) is a pin holder, also called a flower frog or kenzan. It is usually a heavy metal apparatus with upright, closely-spaced tines that help hold flower stems in place. I particularly like pin cups (pin holders that will hold water and can be used as vases themselves). You can find them at:

Dorothy Biddle Service
(www.dorothybiddle.com) and

The Arranger's Market
(www.thearrangersmarket.com).

In addition to offering bulbs that produce large- and medium-sized flowers, bulb specialists Brent and Becky Heath (**Brent and Becky's Bulbs**; www.brentandbeckysbulbs.com) offer hundreds of varieties of small bulbs that provide the little flowers perfect for windowsill arrangements.

To see more windowsill arrangements, visit windowsillarranging.blogspot.com, where Nancy Ross Hugo has been posting her daily windowsill art since May of 2011.

A pin holder nested in this horizontal vase helps hold a Japanese maple branch in position. A pin holder is a device with narrowly spaced, vertical tines that grab stems jammed into them.

ACKNOWLEDGMENTS

By the time they are published, all books owe debts to people other than their authors, but this one was an especially collaborative project.

The biggest contributor was my husband John, who not only read the manuscript (many times) but brought me materials from his own outdoor excursions and never uttered a word of complaint about all the plant debris that accumulated in the kitchen sink.

Other long-term helpers included Joan Kesterman and Joycie Brown whose regular reactions to my blog posts kept me wanting to write for readers like them, and graphic designer Mary Garner-Mitchell, who often dropped her paying work to help me, a friend, when I had page design questions. I aspire to be a friend as generous as Mary. My goddaughter Erin Bishop helped me choose which arrangements to include, garden writer Marty Ross helped me hone what I wanted to say, friend Linda Armstrong provided helpful editing, and fine art photographer Robert Llewellyn spent hours tweaking my photographs. If you think the windowsills in some of my photographs look a little dusty now, you should have seen them before Bob cleaned them up in PhotoShop! Truly, Bob is a wizard and can turn an average photo into a great one.

I'd also like to thank Cathy Dees, editor at St. Lynn's Press, for her careful reading of my manuscript and for her masterful edits. I've worked with lots of editors over a long career, and she is the best. I'll also be forever grateful to publisher Paul Kelly for taking on this project, and to Art Director Holly Rosborough for knowing which of my photos deserved most attention and for listening when I made design suggestions.

What a privilege it has been to have so many good people contributing their insights, expertise, and energy to this project. Thank you all.

ABOUT THE AUTHOR

Nancy Ross Hugo lives, gardens, writes, and arranges flowers in central Virginia. As garden columnist for the *Richmond Times–Dispatch*, education manager for the Lewis Ginter Botanical Garden, and writer for *Horticulture, Fine Gardening, American Forests,* and *Virginia Wildlife,* she learned early how to combine her love for the outdoors with her passion for writing and knack for explaining complex subjects in simple, straightforward language.

Windowsill Art is her fifth book. Her previous books are *Earth Works: Readings for Backyard Gardeners* (University of Virginia Press, 1997), *Remarkable Trees of Virginia* (University of Virginia Press, 2008), *Seeing Trees: Discover the Extraordinary Secret Lives of Everyday Trees* (Timber Press, 2011), and *Trees Up Close: The beauty of bark, leaves, flowers, and seeds* (Timber Press 2014).

Nancy began flower arranging at around age 5, when The Buds, an offshoot of her mother's garden club, let children create tiny flower arrangements before their mothers' meetings.

She never stopped. She has taught floral design to amateurs and experts, practiced floral design professionally, and conducted workshops throughout the mid-Atlantic and on her own farm (where Flower Camp became legendary for its joyful, relaxed, creative approach to floral design). Today, in addition to blogging about the simple windowsill arrangements she creates daily, she lectures on trees, conducts workshops on windowsill art, and explores natural history topics that strike her fancy. Monarch butterflies, birds' nests and Osage orange trees are current obsessions.

Learn more at
www.nancyrosshugo.com.

Other books from St. Lynn's Press:

Slow Flowers
by Debra Prinzing
144 pages
Hardback
ISBN: 978-0-9832726-8-7

Fine Foliage
by Karen Chapman & Christina Salwitz
160 pages
Hardback
ISBN: 978-0-9855622-2-9

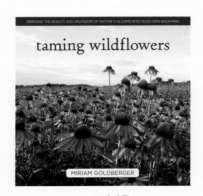

Taming Wildflowers
by Miriam Goldberger
208 pages
Hardback
ISBN: 978-0-9855622-6-7

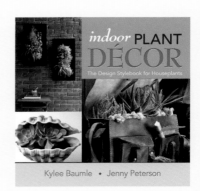

Indoor Plant Decor
by Kylee Baumle & Jenny Peterson
160 pages
Hardback
ISBN: 978-0-9855622-0-5